ORIGAMI

Tips and Techniques

Publications International, Ltd.

Consulting by Sandra Congreve and Katy Higgins

Photography by Christopher Hiltz
Additional images from Shutterstock.com

Louis Weber, CEO
Publications International, Ltd.
8140 Lehigh Avenue
Morton Grove, IL 60053

ISBN: 978-1-63938-279-8

Manufactured in China.

8 7 6 5 4 3 2 1

Table Of Contents

30 Pinwheel
33 Pig
37 Crane
43 Masu Box
47 Bird
50 Bunny
56 Lily
61 Seal

Introduction

Welcome to the world of origami! The art of paper folding is a wonderful way to relax your mind while you keep your fingers busy. Origami models can range from simple to complex, and making origami can be fun for people of all ages. We've included seventeen traditional models here. They start off easy but get more difficult as you go!

The word origami comes from two Japanese words, *ori* meaning folding, and *kami* meaning paper. We don't know exactly when origami began, but by 1680, it was established enough in Japan that a poet could reference a specific butterfly design and expect his audience to be familiar with the concept.

Picking Your Paper

Origami is usually done on a square sheet of paper, with 6" by 6" the standard size for beginners. Usually the paper is colored or patterned on one side and blank on the other. Origami paper is generally fairly thin so that it can be folded and creased easily. Larger paper can be used for more complex models, and paper as small as 1" by 1" can be used to produce adorable miniature models.

One of the delightful things about origami is that you can create beauty simply with paper and your own effort. You don't need expensive specialized tools. In fact, the use of scissors for cutting is discouraged by most origami practitioners! Some people do find a simple tool called a bone folder to be useful for applying sharp creases.

Set Yourself Up for Success

Before you begin each model, look through all the photographs and read the instructions.

When you flatten a fold, first press down in the center and move your finger out to one edge. Then press your finger from the center to the other edge.

DOG

1

Position your paper as a diamond, with the blank side facing up.

2

Bring the top point of the paper down to the bottom point to create a diagonal fold.

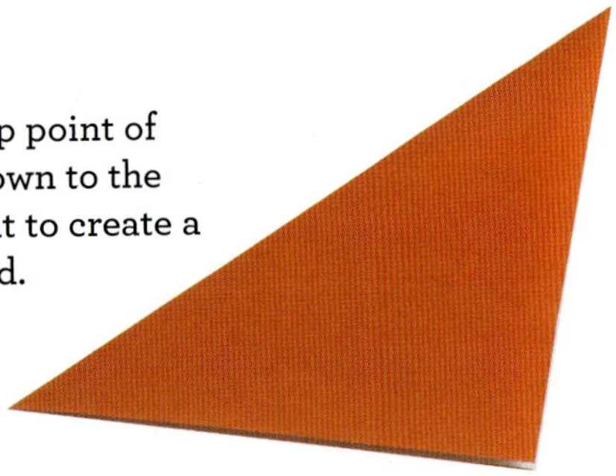

3

Create the dog's ear by folding down one corner of the triangle. The picture here shows one example of where you can place the fold, but it can vary.

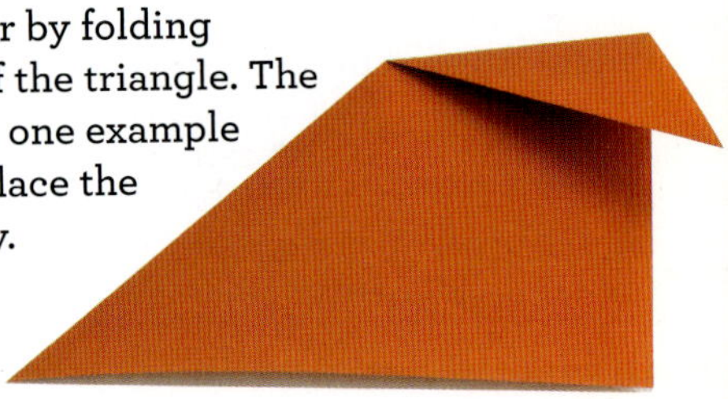

4

Create the dog's other ear in the same way.

5

Turn the dog over and fold up the bottom corner of the paper to create the dog's chin.

6

Turn the dog over to see its face!

Terminology tip!

When you use your eye to create a fold, it is called a *judgment fold*.

Sometimes people use the term *rat fold*. Rat stands for "right about there."

FOX

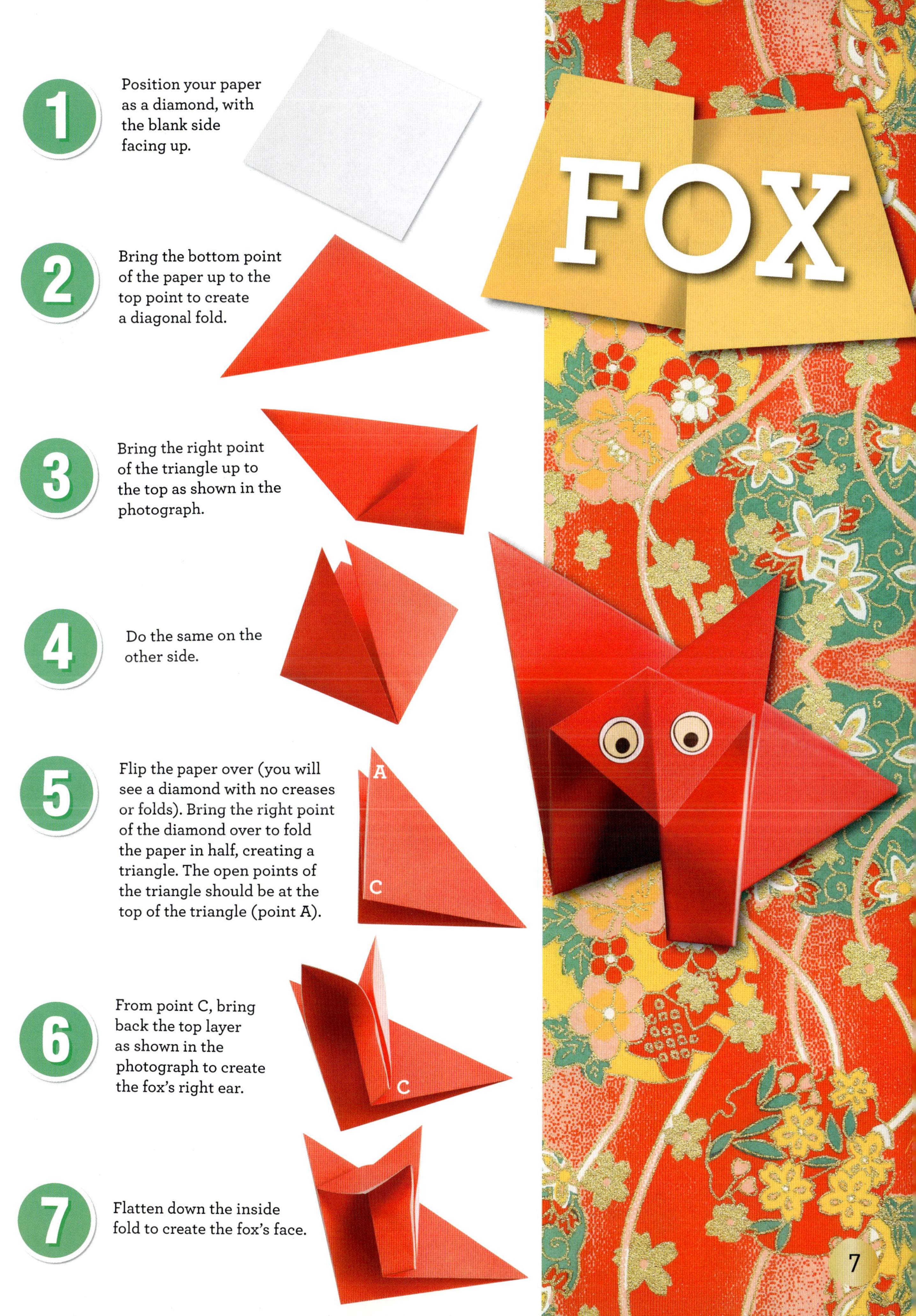

1. Position your paper as a diamond, with the blank side facing up.

2. Bring the bottom point of the paper up to the top point to create a diagonal fold.

3. Bring the right point of the triangle up to the top as shown in the photograph.

4. Do the same on the other side.

5. Flip the paper over (you will see a diamond with no creases or folds). Bring the right point of the diamond over to fold the paper in half, creating a triangle. The open points of the triangle should be at the top of the triangle (point A).

6. From point C, bring back the top layer as shown in the photograph to create the fox's right ear.

7. Flatten down the inside fold to create the fox's face.

PENGUIN

1

Position your paper as a diamond, with the color/pattern facing up.

2

Create a diagonal fold. Then turn the paper sideways, so the top of the triangle now points to the right.

3

Take the top layer of paper and bring it back to the left, creating a fold. This creates the penguin's wing.

Flip the paper over. Take the left corner of the paper and bend it back, creating a fold. This creates the penguin's other wing.

Unfold as shown, leaving the wings in place.

Create the penguin's tail by bringing up the bottom point of the paper.

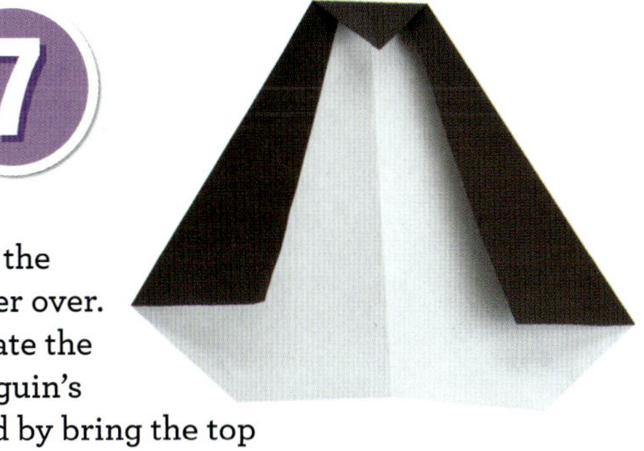

Flip the paper over. Create the penguin's head by bring the top point of the paper down.

8

Flip the paper over and fold it along the center line.

9

Take the penguin's beak and bend it upward to the angle you'd like. Pinch the beak into place.

CAT

1

Position your paper as a diamond, with the blank side facing up.

2

Bring the bottom point of the paper up to the top point to create a diagonal fold.

3

Bring the right point of the triangle over to the left point to create a fold. This creates a guideline fold that you will use later.

4

Open the paper up as seen in the photo.

Fold the top layer of the paper down to meet the bottom edge of the paper.

Fold the paper back up. You will see the fold lines in place.

Bring both layers of the paper down to the guideline fold you just created.

Bring up the right side of the paper to create the cat's ear. Note that you are working from the guideline fold you created in step 3.

Do the same on the left to create the cat's other ear.

Fold up the bottom corner of the paper to create the cat's chin.

Turn the cat over to see its face!

SWAN

1

Position your paper as a diamond, with the blank side facing up.

2

Create a diagonal fold.

3

Open the paper.

4

Bring the bottom corner up to the diagonal fold you created in step 2.

Terminology tip!

When a sequence of folds is used to start many different origami models, it is called a base. The sequence of folds in steps 1 through 5 is called the "kite base."

5

Do the same with the top corner.

6

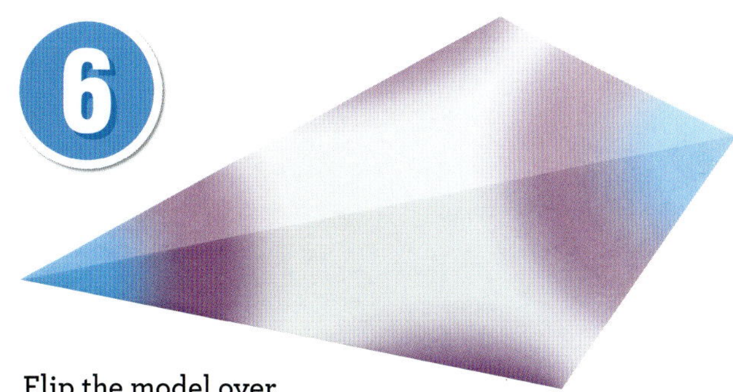

Flip the model over.

7

Narrow the model by bring the bottom corner up to the center crease.

8

Do the same with the top corner.

9

Bring the left corner of the model over to meet the right corner.

10

Create the swan's head by folding back the end point as shown. This is a judgment fold.

11

Fold the model in half.

12

Pull the neck up to where you'd like it.

13

Pinch to set the fold.

Make a swan family by using paper of varying sizes!

SAILBOAT

1

Position your paper as a diamond, with the color/pattern facing up.

2

Bring the bottom point of the paper up to the top point to create a diagonal fold.

3

Open the paper.

4

Bring the left point of the paper over to create another diagonal fold, then open the paper.

5

Flip the paper over so the blank side faces up.

6

Create a fold along the center line of the paper, the open the paper.

7

Create a fold along the perpendicular line, then open the paper. You should see the folds as shown here.

8

Take one corner and fold it in to the center crease.

9

Do the same with the opposite corner.

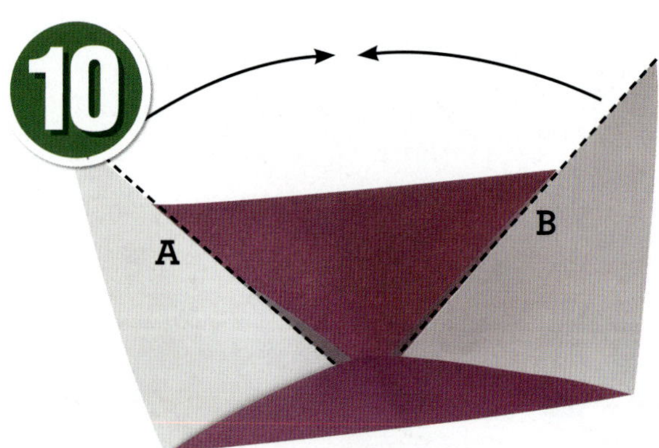

10

Take the left and right points and bring them upward. Dotted lines A and B will meet.

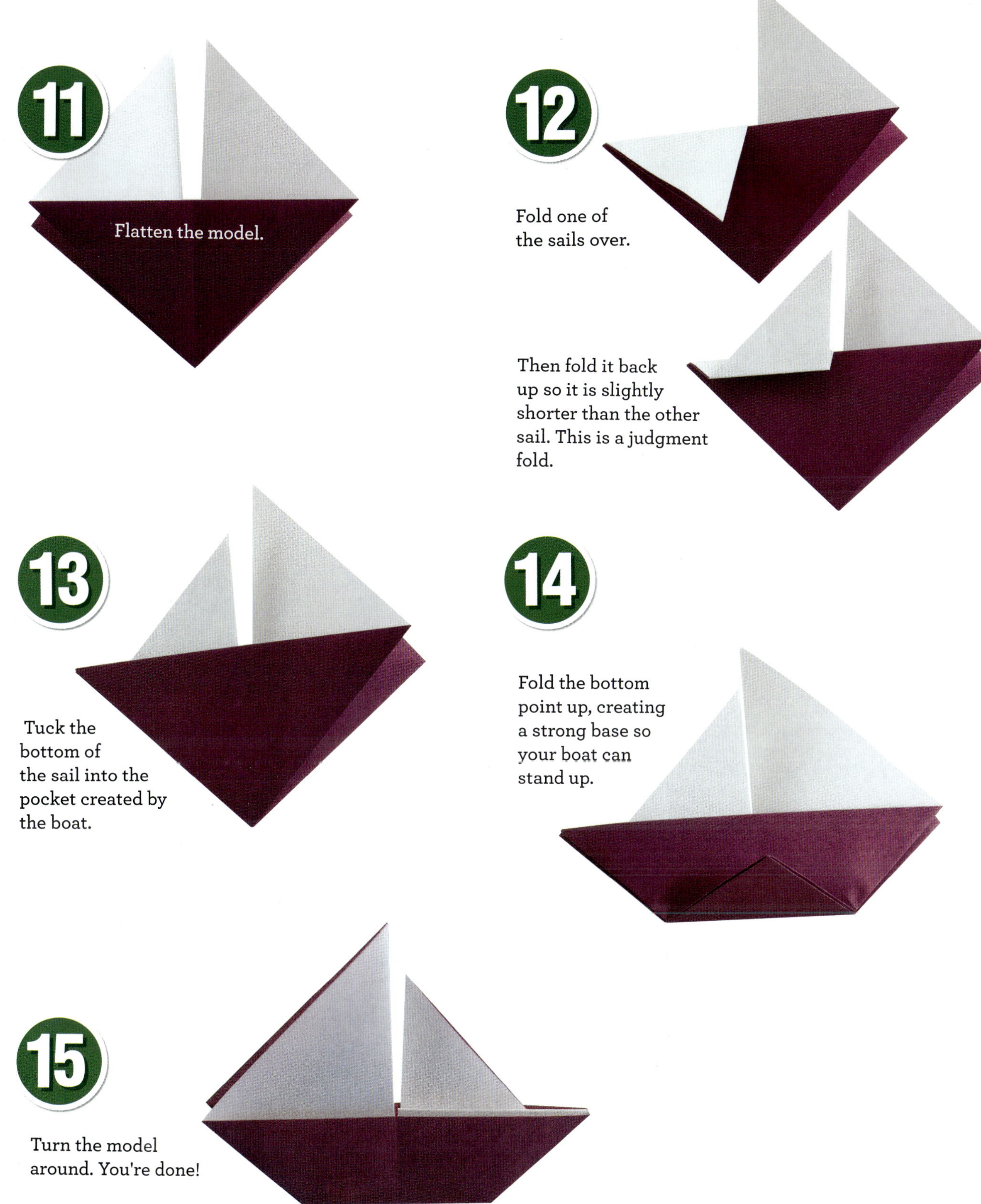
11
Flatten the model.
12
Fold one of
the sails over.
Then fold it back
up so it is slightly
shorter than the other
sail. This is a judgment
fold.
13
Tuck the
bottom of
the sail into the
pocket created by
the boat.
14
Fold the bottom
point up, creating
a strong base so
your boat can
stand up.
15
Turn the model
around. You're done!

BALLOON

Position your paper as a square, with the color/pattern facing up.

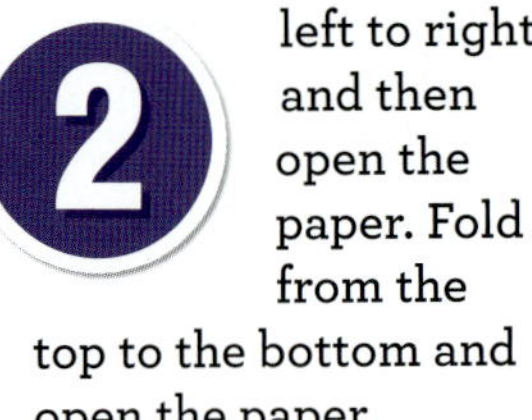

Fold from left to right and then open the paper. Fold from the top to the bottom and open the paper.

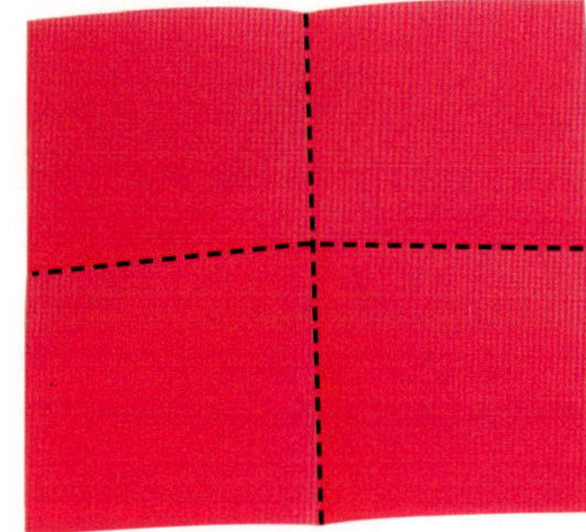

Flip the paper over.

4

Create folds along the diagonals, then open the paper up.

Terminology tip!

The sequence of opening steps is called the "balloon base."

Bring the sides of the paper in *(picture A)* and then flatten down as shown. *(picture B)*

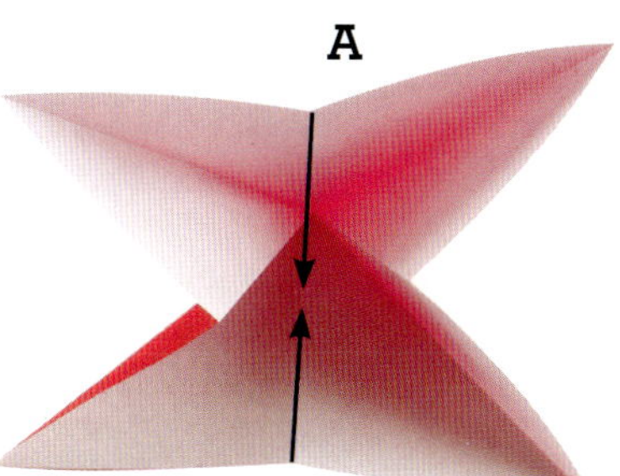

Take the right corner and bring it to the top point.

Do the same with the left corner.

Flip the paper over and perform the same steps on the other side.

Take the right corner and fold in to the center line.

Do the same on the other side.

Flip the paper over and repeat the same steps on the other side.

The open points of the model should be at the top. Take the top layer of the top point and fold it down to make a triangle.

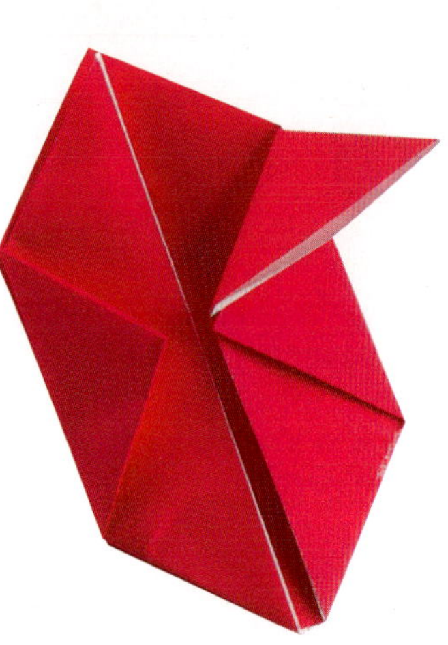

13

The right side of the triangle folds again, and then the small triangle is tucked into the pocket.

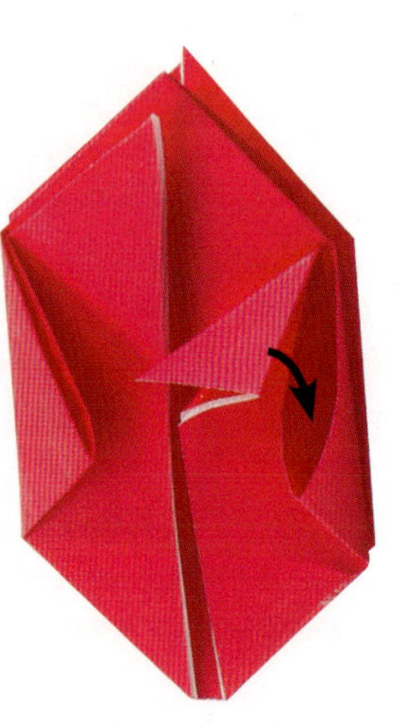

14

Perform steps 12 and 13 on the opposite side, and then flip the model over and perform the same actions on the other side.

15

Blow gently into the opening at the end to inflate your balloon. It can also be filled with water.

TULIP & STEM

Let's start with the tulip's stem.

1

Position the paper as a diamond, with the blank side facing up.

2

Create a fold along the diagonal, then open the paper.

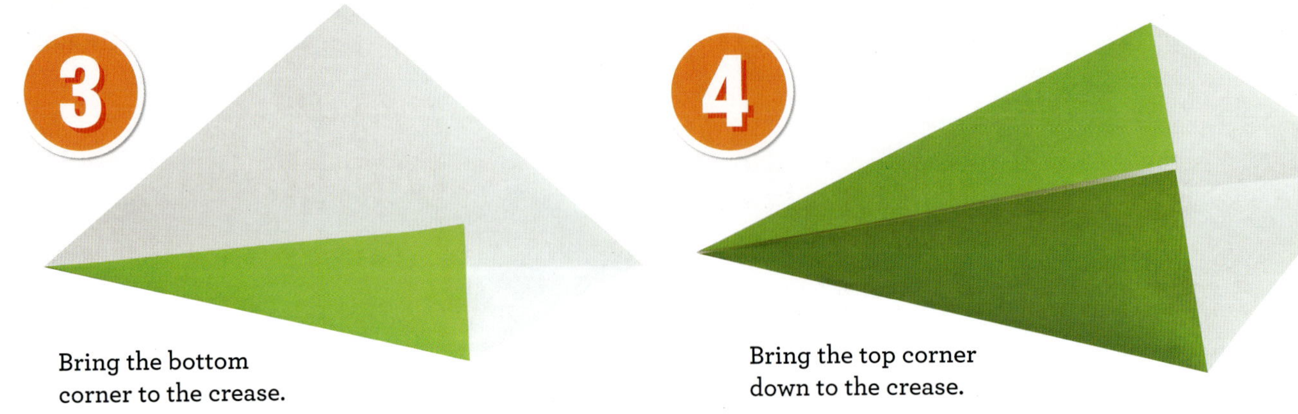

Bring the bottom corner to the crease.

Bring the top corner down to the crease.

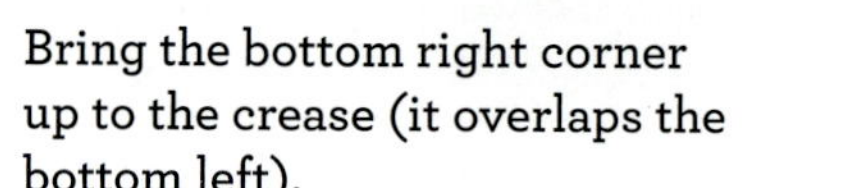

Bring the bottom right corner up to the crease (it overlaps the bottom left).

Do the same with the top right corner.

Narrow your tulip stem by folding the bottom edge up to the center.

Do the same with the top.

Take the narrow point, and fold it to meet the top point.

Fold the model in half.

Bring the inside stem out a bit and pinch to set the fold.

Technique tip!

Put a penny in each inside pocket to help the tulip stem stand upright.

Now let's go on to the flower!

Position the paper as a square, with the color/pattern facing up.

2

Fold from left to right and then open the paper. Fold from the top to the bottom and open the paper.

3

Turn the paper over. Fold along each diagonal, then open the paper.

4

Bring the sides in and flatten the model as shown.

5

Take the left corner of the top layer and bring it up to the top point. Then do the same to the right corner.

Flip the model over. Bring the left corner up to the top point, and then do the same to the right corner.

7

Bring the right side of the top layer up and flip it over to the left side, as if you were turning the page in a book. In the end, you will see a diamond shape without any open edges.

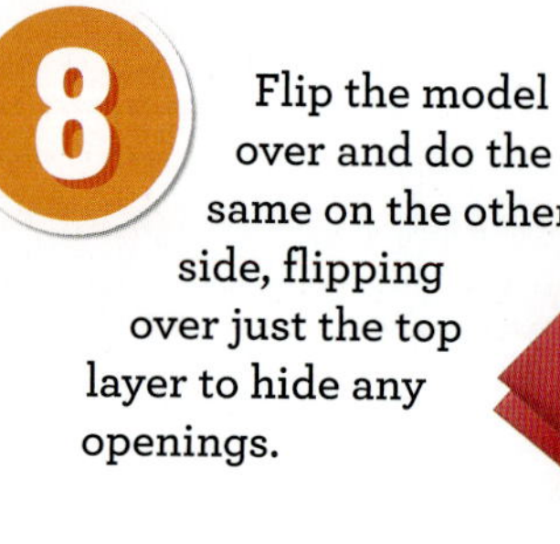

8

Flip the model over and do the same on the other side, flipping over just the top layer to hide any openings.

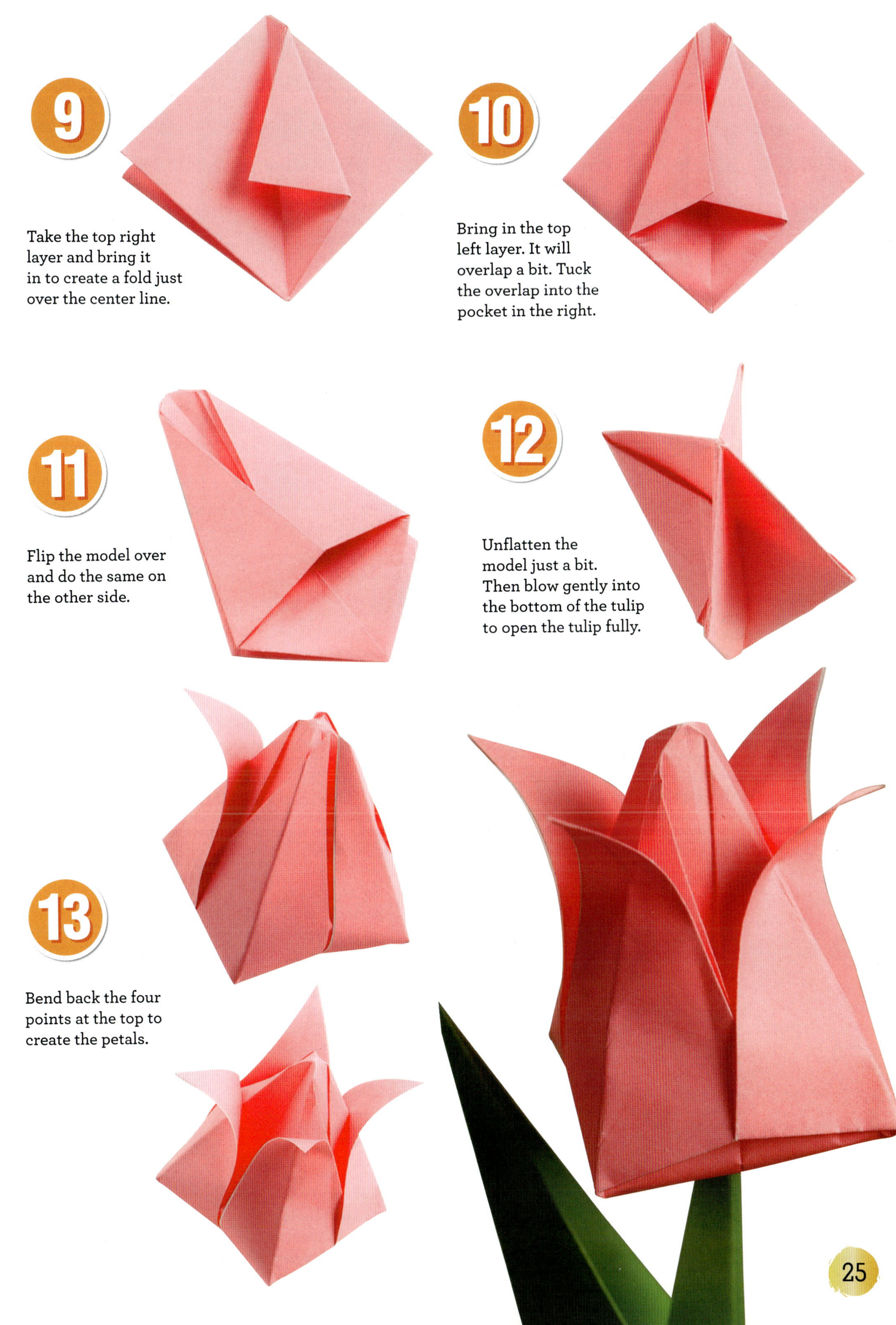
9
Take the top right layer and bring it in to create a fold just over the center line.
10
Bring in the top left layer. It will overlap a bit. Tuck the overlap into the pocket in the right.
11
Flip the model over and do the same on the other side.
12
Unflatten the model just a bit. Then blow gently into the bottom of the tulip to open the tulip fully.
13
Bend back the four points at the top to create the petals.

JUMPING FROG

1

Position your paper as a square, with the blank side facing up.

2

Bring the left side of the paper over to make a rectangle.

3

Bring the top left corner of the rectangle over to the right edge of the paper.

Unfold to see the crease you just created.

Do the same with the right corner.

Flip the paper over. Bring the top of the paper down and create a fold. The fold should cross the intersection of your two diagonal creases.

Then unfold to see the crease you just created and flip the paper over again.

Touch the center point as shown in the picture, and then bring in the sides to create a triangular shape.

Bring up the bottom half of the model to the bottom of the triangle.

Bring the left side of the bottom layer in to the center.

Do the same on the right.

Fold the tip of the triangle up as shown. This creates the frog's front leg.

Do the same on the other side.

Fold the top layer of the bottom right corner of the model as shown. Do the same on the other side.

Fold the frog in half, bringing the top layer down to the bottom corner.

Flip the frog over so that you're seeing the square of its back.

Bring the bottom of the square back and fold it in half.

Flip your frog over. Press the base of the frog's back and release to make your frog hop!

Materials tip!

This model works well and hops well with a rectangular index card. Just start at step 3!

PINWHEEL

1

Position your paper with the color/pattern facing up.

2

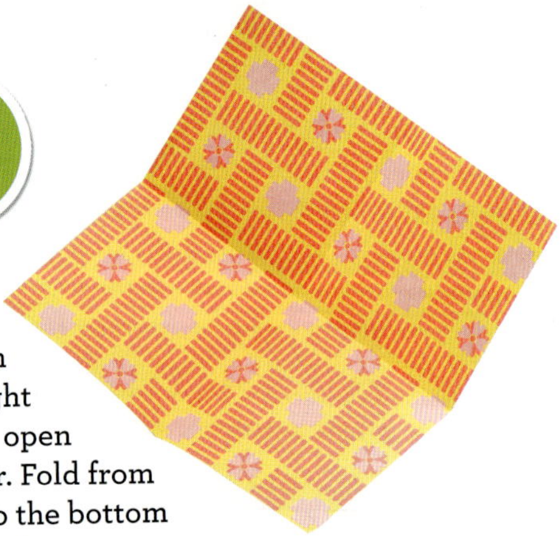

Fold from left to right and then open the paper. Fold from the top to the bottom and open the paper.

3

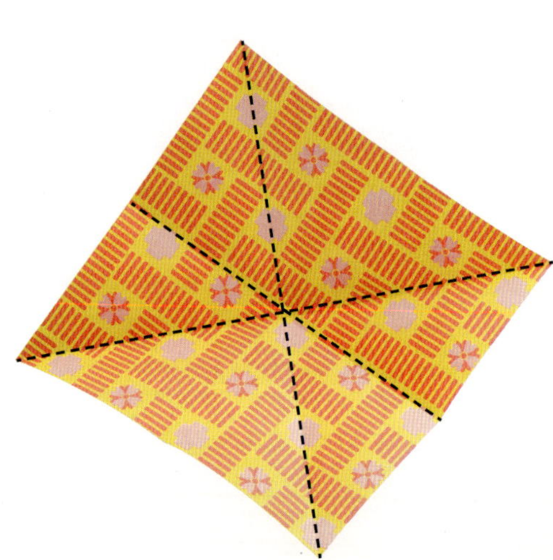

Create two more folds along the diagonal lines. Open the paper; you should see the fold lines as shown in the picture.

4

Bring one corner of the paper in to the center of the paper.

5

Do the same with the other three corners.

Terminology tip!

This is called the "blintz fold" or "cushion fold."

6

Open the paper back up.

7

Flip it over.

8

Fold each edge to the center line, then unfold the paper.

Do the same with the opposite edges. Then unfold the paper.

Fold over two edges as shown, leaving the corner out.

Now flatten the corner as shown.

Technique tip!

As you work, look ahead to the following steps before you make a fold.

Moving clockwise, do the same for the next corner.

13

The last two folds will be flattened in one step.

PIG

1 Position the paper as a square, with the blank side facing up.

2 Fold the bottom to the top to create a rectangle.

3 Then unfold.

4 Fold the top and the bottom edges in to the center.

Bring the left edge over, folding the paper in half.

Then unfold the last fold.

Fold each side into the center.

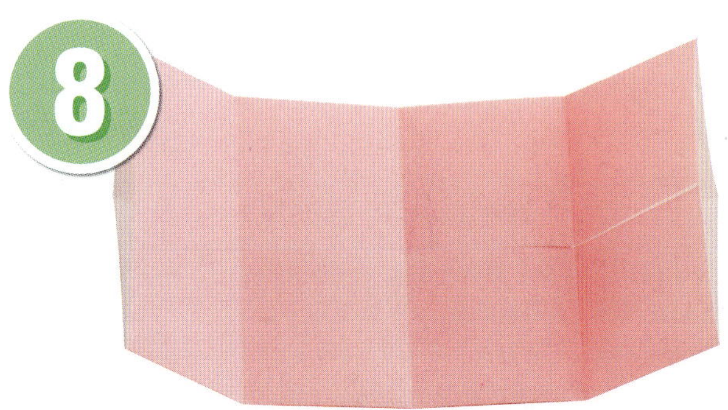

Then open the last folds.

Fold each corner in to the center line.

Unfold the top right corner. Then bring over point A as shown.

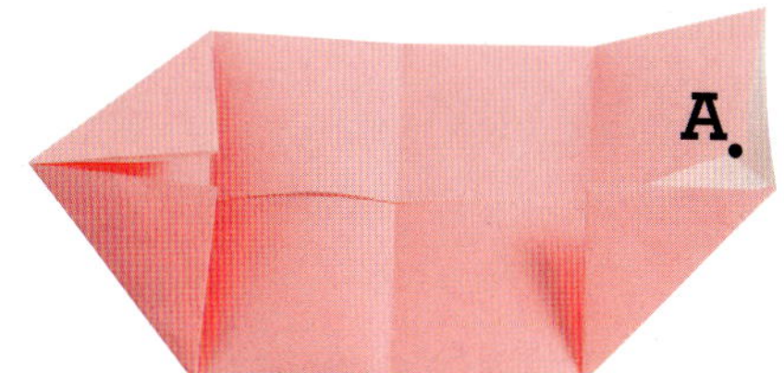

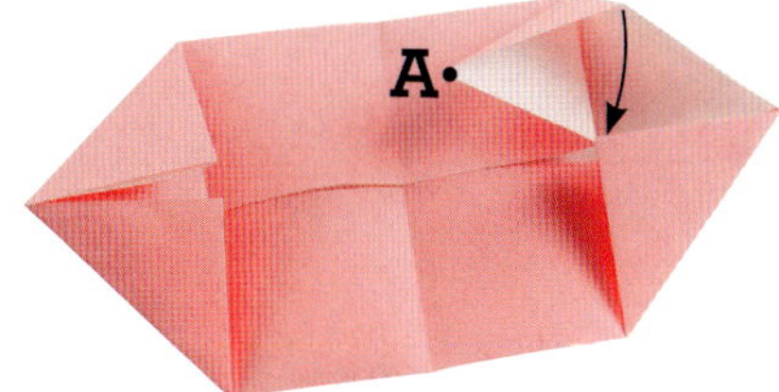

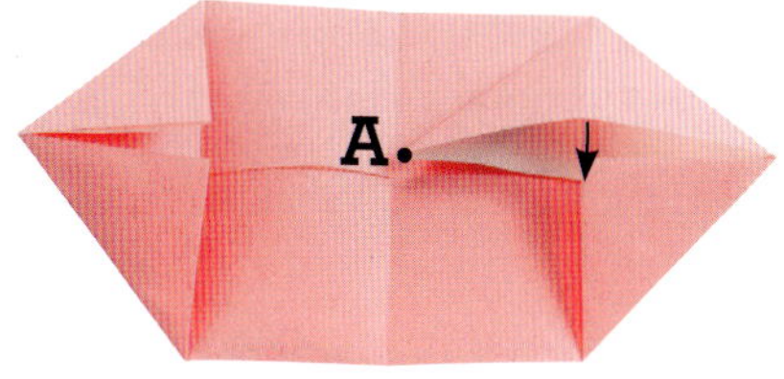

Do the same for the other three corners.

Fold the model in half along the center. The triangular folds you just created are on the outside.

Turn the model over as shown.

Take the inside of each triangle and fold as shown to create two of the pig's legs.

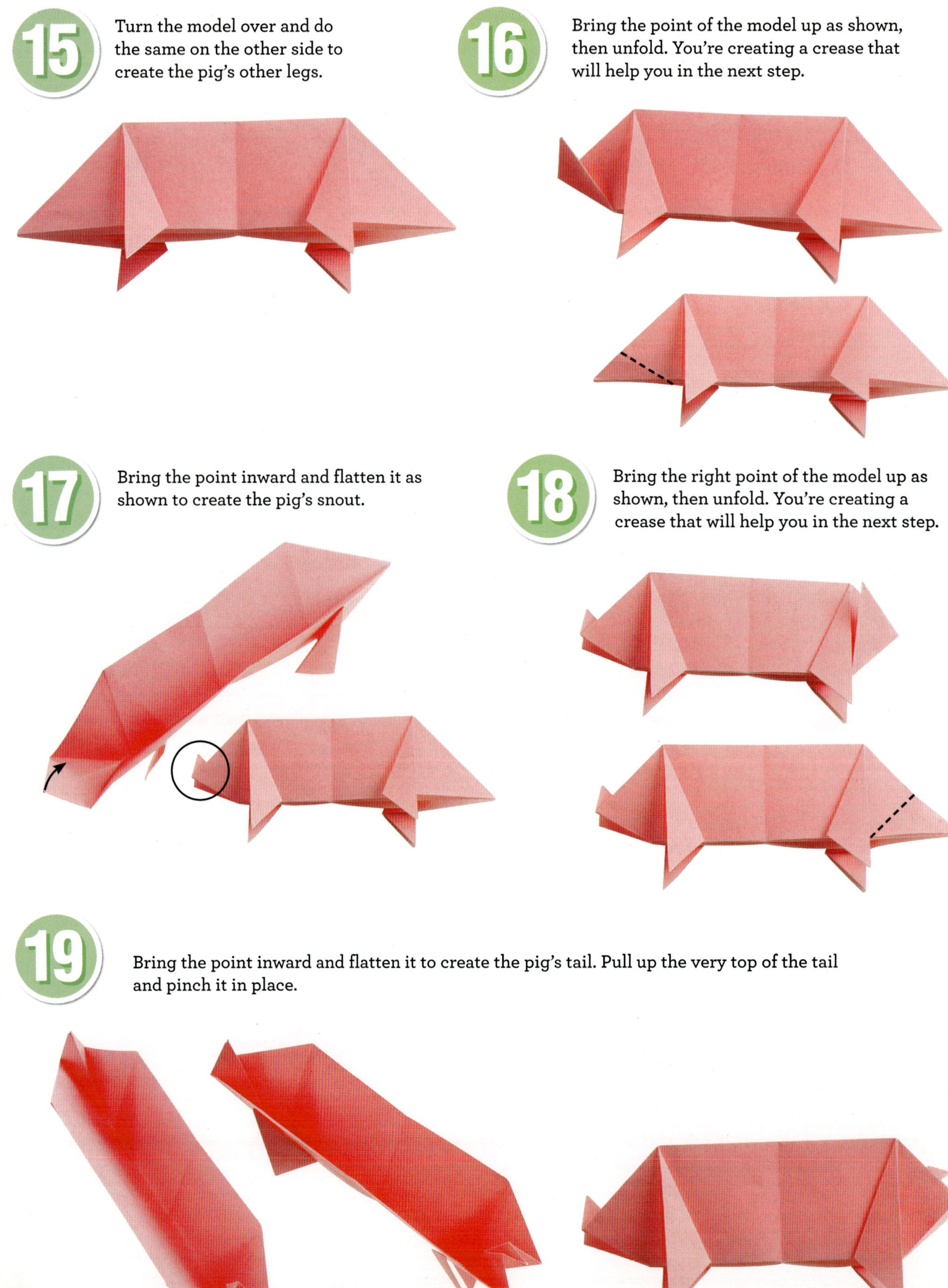

15 Turn the model over and do the same on the other side to create the pig's other legs.

16 Bring the point of the model up as shown, then unfold. You're creating a crease that will help you in the next step.

17 Bring the point inward and flatten it as shown to create the pig's snout.

18 Bring the right point of the model up as shown, then unfold. You're creating a crease that will help you in the next step.

19 Bring the point inward and flatten it to create the pig's tail. Pull up the very top of the tail and pinch it in place.

CRANE

1

Position your paper as a diamond, with the color/pattern facing up.

2

Create folds along the diagonals.

3

Turn the paper over.

4

Fold from left to right, and then from top to bottom.

Bring in the sides of the model so that the four corners meet.

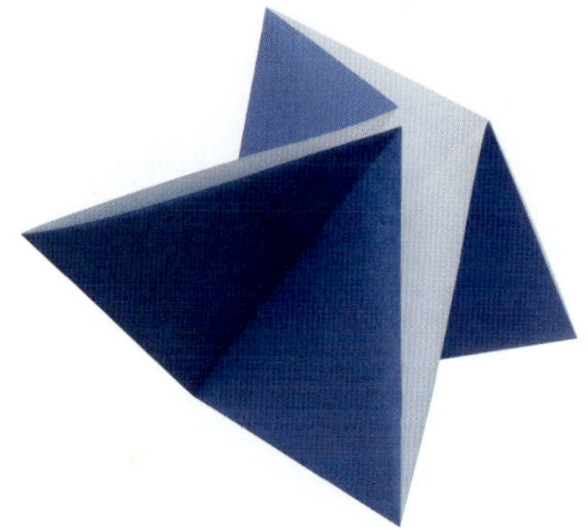

Flatten the model. The open points face downward.

Bring the top left layer in to the center crease. Do the same with the top right layer.

Fold the top point downward.

Unfold the model to see the creases created in the last two steps.

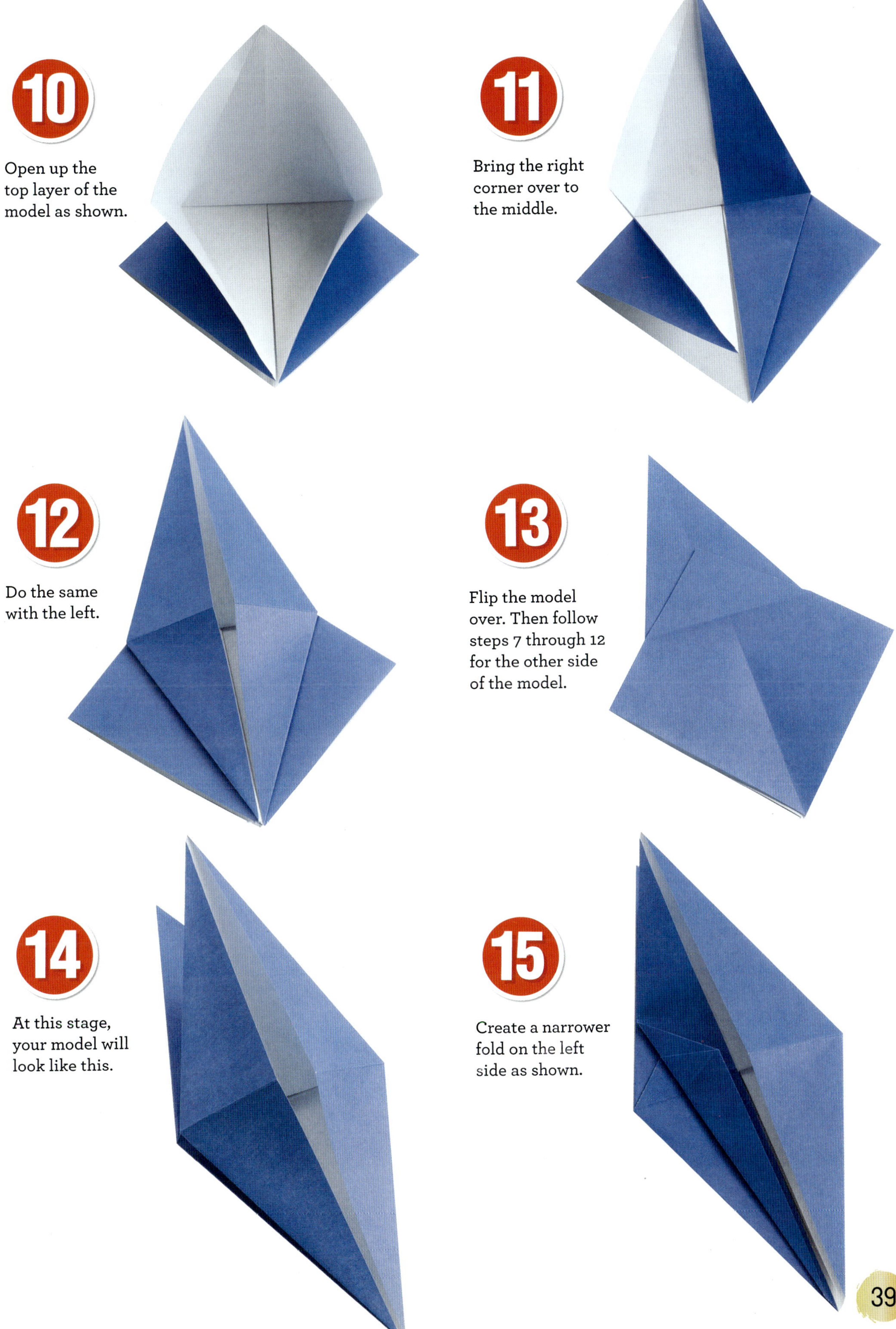

10

Open up the top layer of the model as shown.

11

Bring the right corner over to the middle.

12

Do the same with the left.

13

Flip the model over. Then follow steps 7 through 12 for the other side of the model.

14

At this stage, your model will look like this.

15

Create a narrower fold on the left side as shown.

Do the same on the right.

Flip the model over and follow steps 15 and 16 on the other side.

Fold the bottom point of the model upward as shown.

Do the same on the other side. In steps 18 and 19, you are creating creases that you will use in later steps.

Bring down the points.

Bring the point upward and tuck it on the inside of the model. You are bringing it underneath the top layer but above the bottom layer.

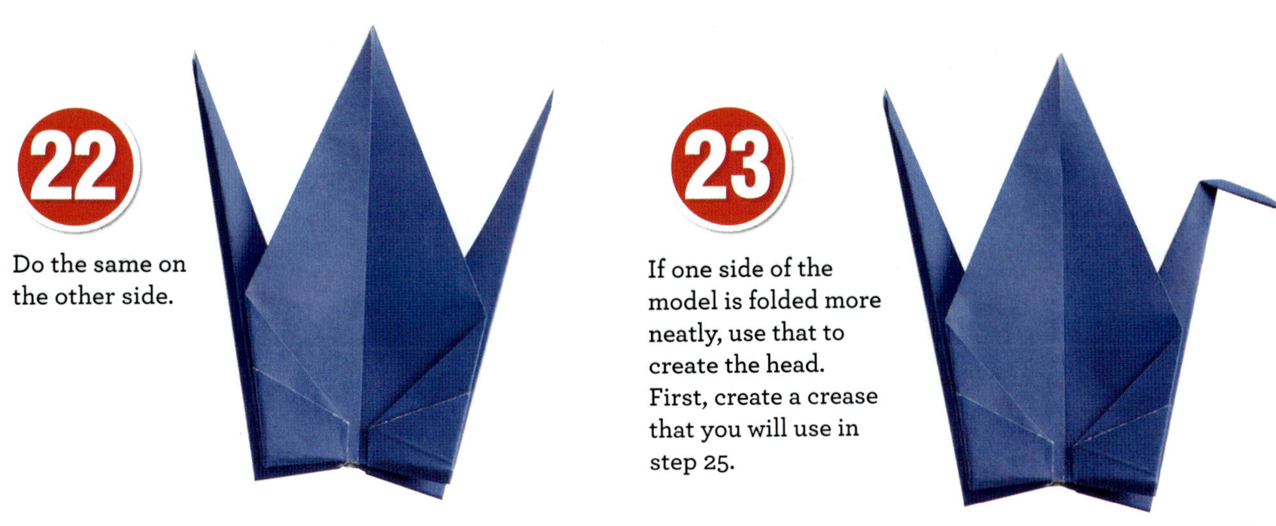

22

Do the same on the other side.

23

If one side of the model is folded more neatly, use that to create the head. First, create a crease that you will use in step 25.

24

Unfold.

25

Tuck the head down as shown.

26

Bend down the wings.

Once you get the hang of making the crane, make it miniature! You can even use your origami cranes in jewelry.

You may have heard the legend that folding 1,000 origami cranes will bring you good luck or grant a wish. A group of 1,000 origami cranes is called a *senbazuru*. The cranes are strung together.

MASU BOX

1

Begin with the paper as a square, with the blank side facing up.

2

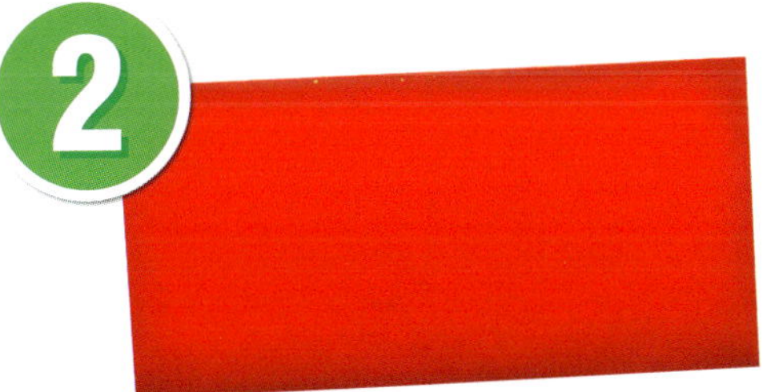

Fold in half, creasing from edge to edge.

3

Unfold the paper.

4

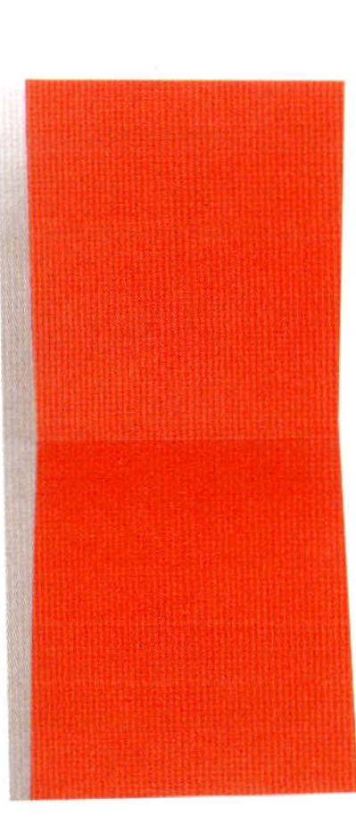

Fold edge to edge in the opposite direction.

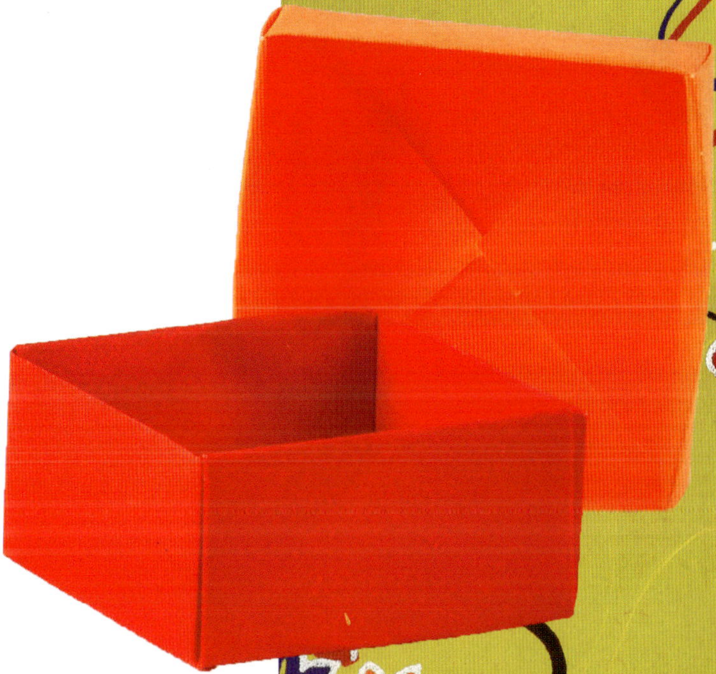

Unfold to show the creases.

Fold one corner in towards the center.

Fold the opposite corner in towards the center.

Repeat with the remaining corners. This is the blintz crease, also used with the Pinwheel.

Fold one edge into the center.

Fold the opposite edge into the center.

Unfold as shown.

Rotate the box. Fold the other edge into the center.

Fold the final edge into the center.

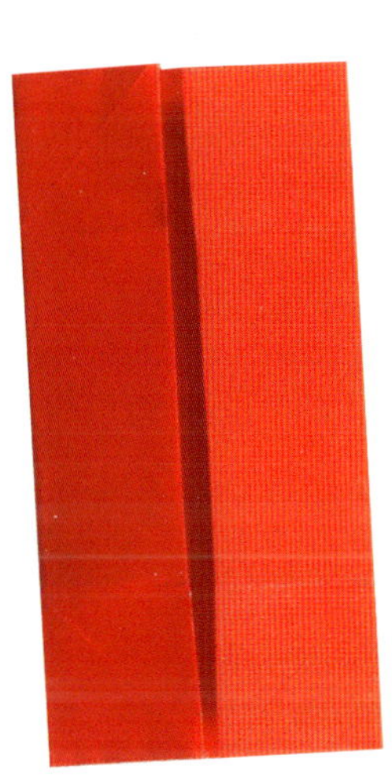

Unfold as shown and pull out the edges.

Lift up the sides so that the creases collapse inward. The model will start to become 3D and not lie flat.

Fold down the top corner flap onto existing creases, into the center.

Repeat the last 2 steps with the remaining flap. A dot of tape will help keep the flaps down.

18

Create the lid of the box in the same way. However, when you reach step 9, don't fold quite to the center. Repeat with the top edge. Continue completing the masu box model.

19

Your box and lid now fit together!

Place a pinwheel on top of your box to decorate it! Use a smaller size sheet of origami for the pinwheel.

BIRD

1

Begin with a square, blank side up.

2

Fold in half, corner to corner, then unfold.

3

Fold bottom right edge to the center line. Repeat on the left.

4

Turn the model over.

5

Fold down the corner, starting at the two points, aligning the tip with the center line.

Turn the model over.

7

Fold down top right corner to meet the center line.

8

Repeat with top left corner.

9

Unfold right corner, opening paper like a pocket.

10

Use existing creases to pinch and flatten as shown.

11

Repeat on the left side.

12

Fold up right and left tips to create feet.

13

Fold bottom tip to meet the point, as shown.

14

Create a small crimp by folding the tip back down.

15

Fold the model in half along the center line, right to left, and rotate.

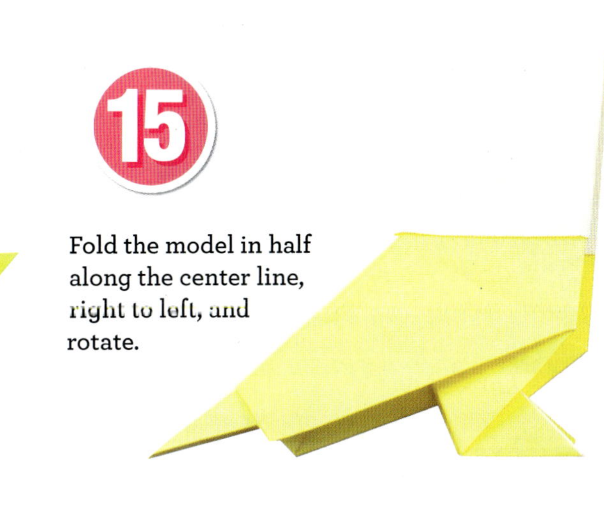

16

Precrease the head by folding down the tip.

17

Unfold tip and inside reverse fold to create the head.

BUNNY

1

Begin with the color/pattern side facing up.

2

Fold in half, corner to corner.

3

Unfold.

4

Fold in half, corner to corner.

Unfold and turn the paper over.

Fold in half, edge to edge, and unfold.

Repeat on the other edge.

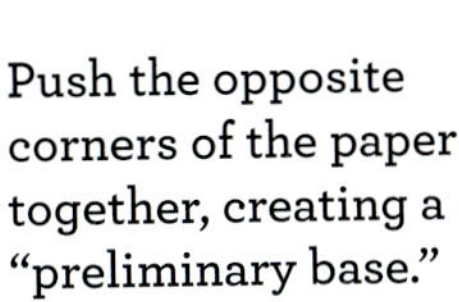

Push the opposite corners of the paper together, creating a "preliminary base."

Terminology tip!

The preliminary base is the bread-and-butter of the origami world. It looks like a square that is ¼ the size of the original paper, and has a total of 4 flaps.

Flatten, with the open edges on the bottom, and the closed tip on top.

Fold the right edge to the center, top layer only.

Repeat on the left side.

12

Repeat steps 10-11 on the back.

13

Unfold steps 10-11 and use the existing creases to “petal fold” by opening the paper and pushing it inside.

14

Repeat on the back.

15

Adjust so that one of the top flaps is facing up, and flap on the other side is facing down, as shown.

16

Fold the model in half.

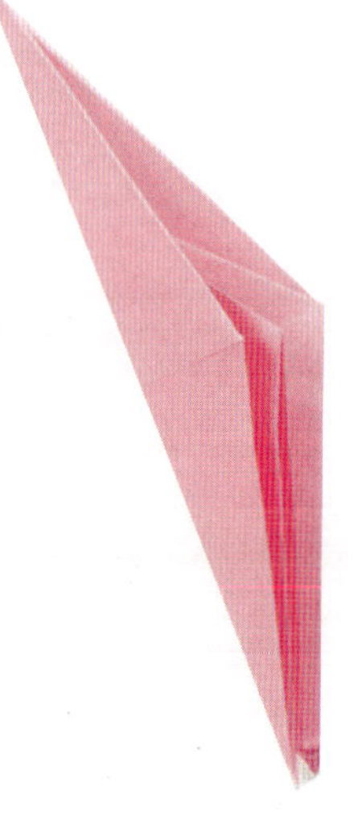

17

Rotate the model so that the side with multiple layers is at the top.

18

Fold all layers down and to the right, aligning with the horizontal crease seen in previous step.

19

Unfold step 18 and open the model.

20

Use the creases made in step 18 to "outside reverse fold," closing the model.

21

Begin to peel one layer away from the others.

22

Fold down the head using the layer from step 21.

Blunt the nose by tucking the tip inside.

Fold the right tip to meet the left side of the model.

Unfold, and reverse fold inside the model.

Crimp fold part of the tip back out, forming the tail.

Blunt the tip of the tail by folding the tip inside.

Open the ears by inserting finger or straw into the ear pockets.

You're done!

Make it miniature!

Use different sizes of paper to make a bunny family!

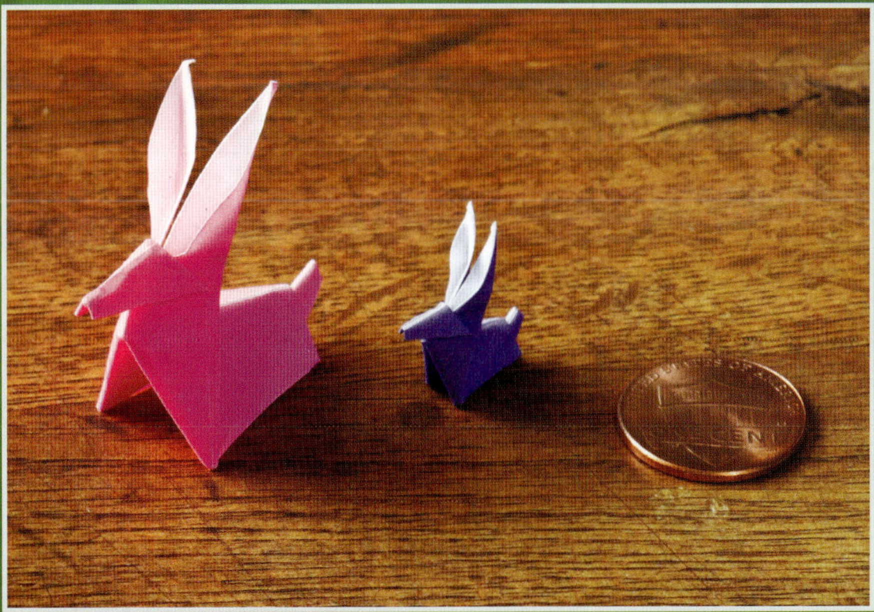

LILY

1 Begin with the color/pattern side facing up.

2 Fold in half, corner to corner, and unfold. Repeat on the other side.

3 Turn the paper over, fold in half edge to edge, and unfold. Repeat on the other side.

4 Using existing creases, push the corners together to create a "preliminary base."

5

Lift one flap on the right.

6

Squash fold.

7

Flatten.

8

Repeat with the other three flaps.

9

Fold in both edges on top layer, as shown.

10

Unfold last step and perform a "petal fold": Open the flap like a pocket and push in the paper.

Flatten.

Fold down the triangle tip.

Repeat steps 9-12 on the other 3 flaps.

Rotate the model 90 degrees.

Fold the top right layer to the left, like folding the page of a book.

Repeat on the other side.

Fold bottom right edge to align with the center crease.

Repeat on the left side.

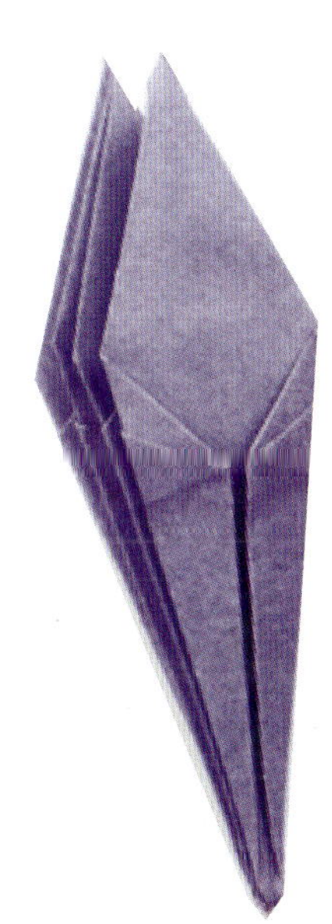

Repeat steps 17-18 on the back, then the other two sides of the model.

Fold down a petal.

Repeat so all four petals are open.

Curl the petals using a straw or pencil.

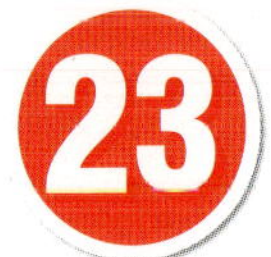

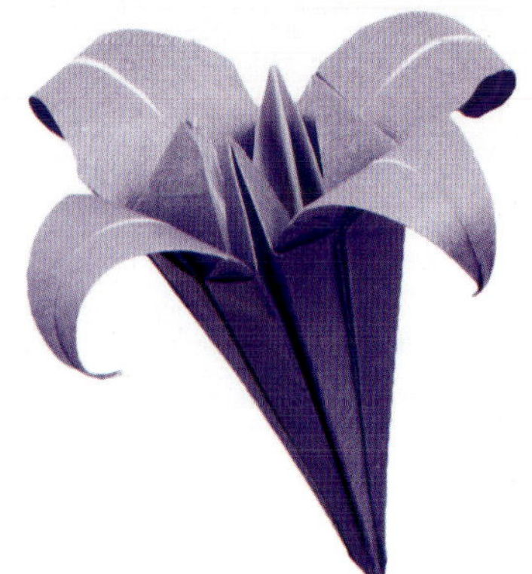

23

You're done!

24

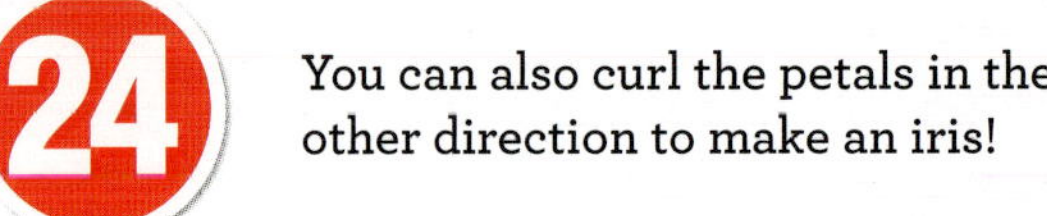

You can also curl the petals in the other direction to make an iris!

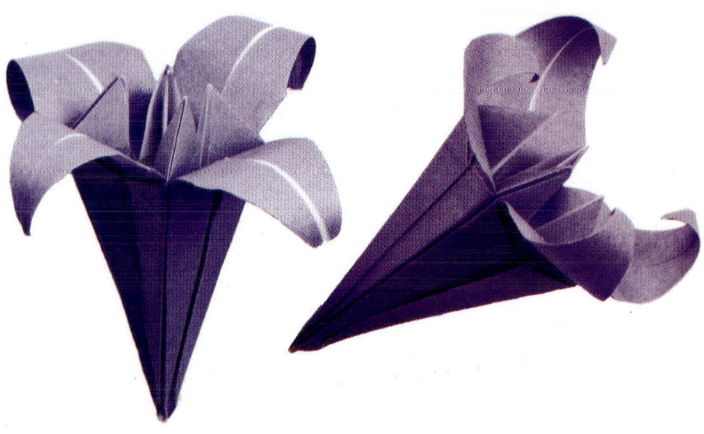

You can use the stem from the tulip model for your lily!
Cut a tiny hole at the bottom of the model to fit the stem.

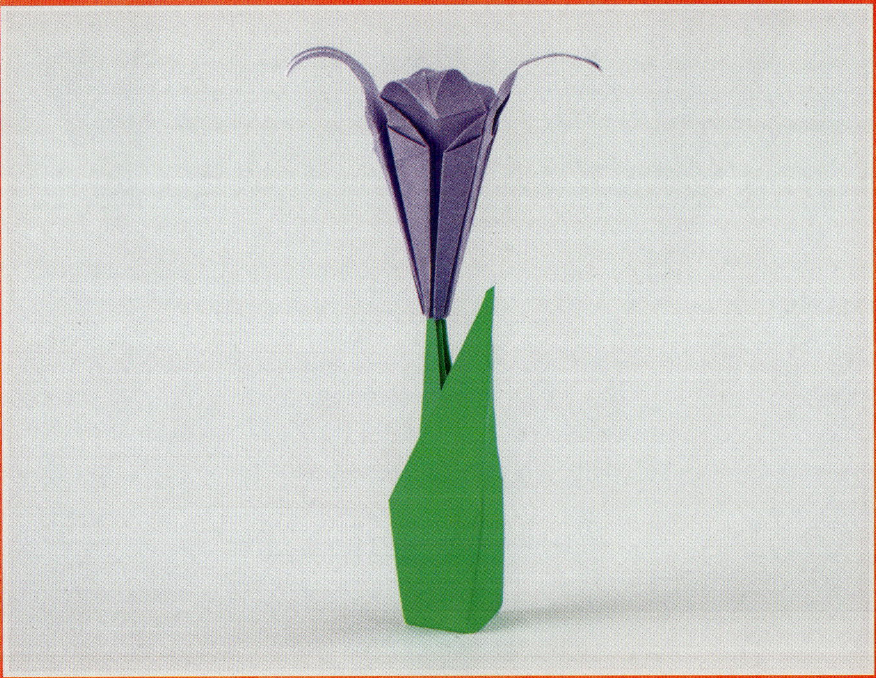

SEAL

Begin with a square, with the blank side facing up.

2

Fold in half, corner to corner.

3

Unfold.

Fold bottom right edge to align with the center line. This is called an "angle bisector" fold, dividing the angle in half.

5

Repeat with bottom left edge.

6

Turn the model over.

7

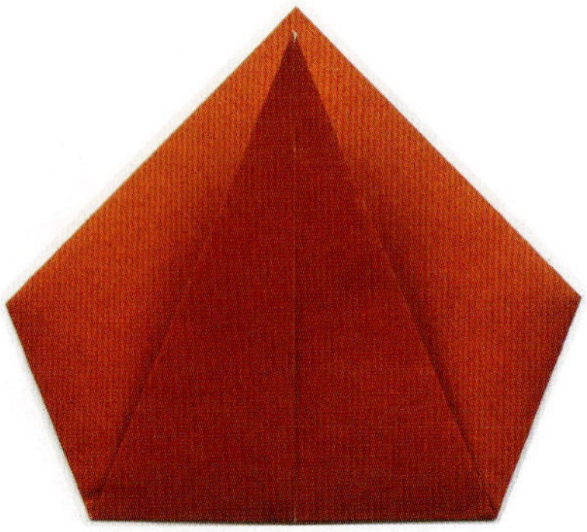

Fold bottom tip to the top.

8

Turn model over and rotate, as shown.

9

Open the bottom flap like a pocket.

10

Flatten the flap.

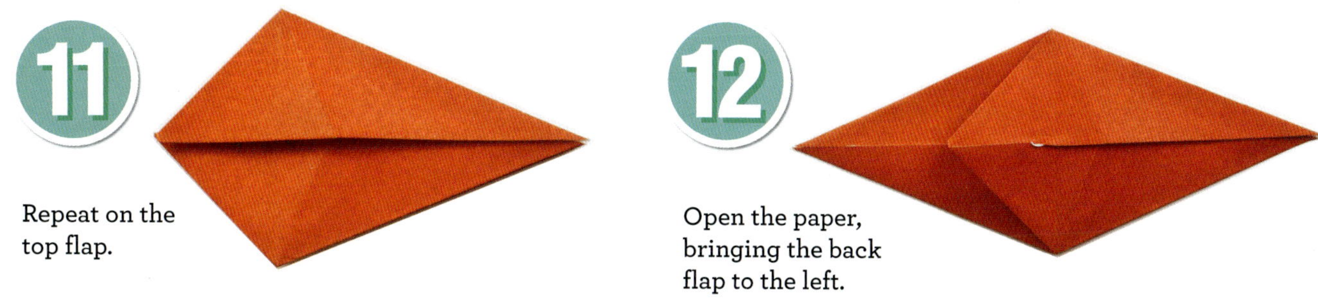

Repeat on the top flap.

Open the paper, bringing the back flap to the left.

Fold the model in half along the center crease

Fold right side up, aligning bottom edge with top tip (creating a 90 degree angle.)

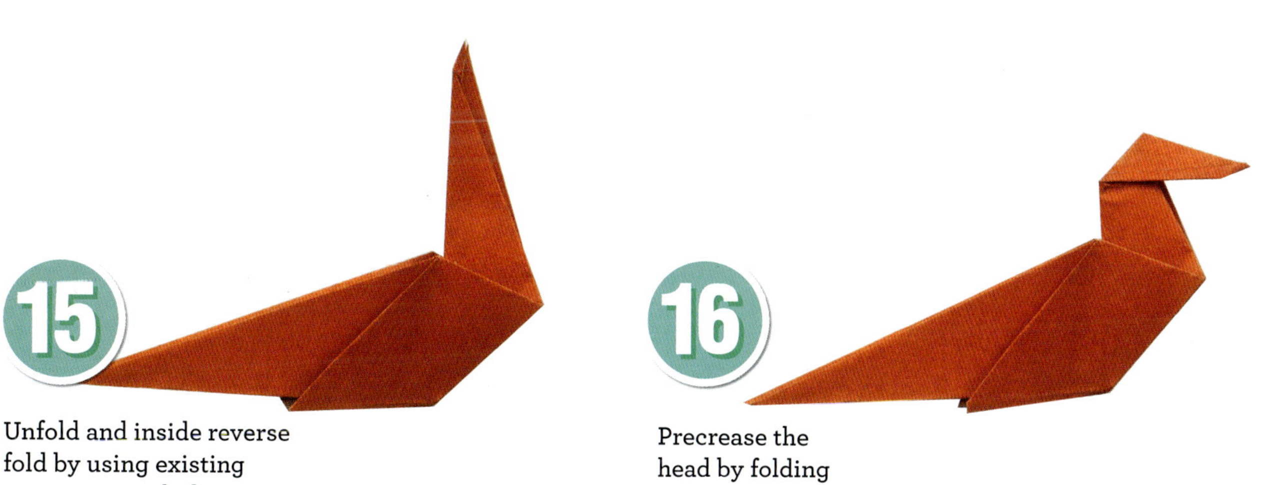

Unfold and inside reverse fold by using existing creases to push the paper inside the model.

Precrease the head by folding down the tip.

17

Unfold tip and inside reverse fold by tucking the paper inside the model.

18

Blunt the nose the same way, and tuck the tip inside.

19

Fold the flap to the front, creating a flipper. Repeat on the other side.

20

Precrease the tail by folding tip up.

21

Inside reverse fold!

22

You're done!